What are Taxes?

Baron Bedesky

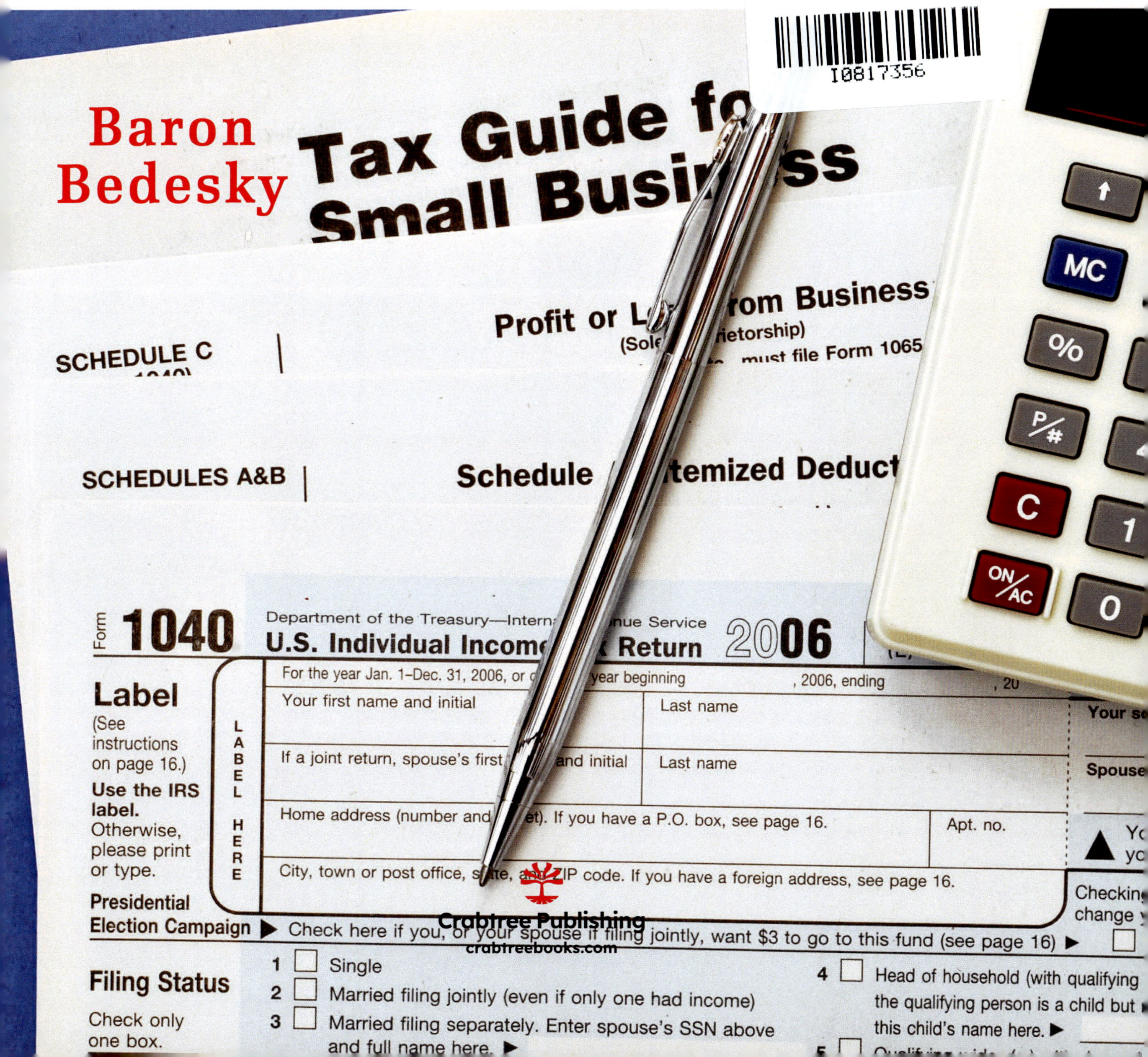

Crabtree Publishing
crabtreebooks.com

Crabtree Publishing

crabtreebooks.com 800-387-7650

In Canada: We acknowledge the financial support of the Government of Canada through the Canada Book Fund for our publishing activities.

Author: Baron Bedesky
Coordinating editor: Chester Fisher
Series editor: Scholastic Ventures
Editor: Amanda Bishop
Proofreaders: Adrianna Morganelli, Crystal Sikkens
Project editor: Robert Walker
Print and production coordinator: Katherine Kantor
Prepress technician: Katherine Kantor
Project manager: Santosh Vasudevan (Q2AMEDIA)
Art direction: Dibakar Acharjee (Q2AMEDIA)
Cover design: Ranjan Singh (Q2AMEDIA)
Design: Ruchi Sharma (Q2AMEDIA)
Photo research: Himanshu Chaudhary (Q2AMEDIA)

Hardcover 978-0-7787-4257-9
Paperback 978-0-7787-4262-3
Ebook (pdf) 978-0-7787-8970-3

Printed in Canada/062024/CP20240604

Published in Canada
Crabtree Publishing
616 Welland Avenue
St. Catharines, Ontario
L2M 5V6

Published in the United States
Crabtree Publishing
347 Fifth Avenue
Suite 1402-145
New York, NY 10016

Photographs:
Alamy: The London Art Archive: p. 6, 9; North Wind Picture Archives: p. 8, 11
AP images: Charles Dharapak: p. 28; Tom Strattman: p. 27
DefenseImagery.mil: p. 22
Dreamstime: Kcphotos : p. 13; Lilalila: p. 16; Logoboom: p. 18; Rramirez125: p. 17; Velefante: p. 5
Flickr: Jesse Engelkins: p. 25
Fotolia: Deborah Clague: p. 7
Istockphoto: Ralph125: p. 4; Igor Vorobyov: cover (top right)
Library of Congress: Alexander Gardner: p. 10
LOC prints and publications: p. 20
NOAA: p. 23
Q2A Media Art Bank: p. 24
Shutterstock: Sharon D: p. 1; Elnur: p. 26; Iivanastar: cover (top left); Timur Kulgarin: p. 15; Massimiliano Lamagna: p. 21; Chee-Onn Leong: p. 29; Phecsone: cover (bottom left); Rj lerich: p. 19; Scott Rothstein: p. 14
Stockxpert: Bcnewell: p. 12; cmcderm1: cover (bottom right)

Library and Archives Canada Cataloguing in Publication
Bedesky, Baron
What are taxes? / Baron Bedesky.

(Economics in action)
Includes index.
ISBN 978-0-7787-4257-9 (bound).--
ISBN 978-0-7787-4262-3 (pbk.)

1. Taxation--United States--Juvenile literature. I. Title.
II. Series: Economics in action (St. Catherines, Ont.)

HJ2381.B43 2008 j336.200973 C2008-903711-1

Library of Congress Cataloging-in-Publication Data
Bedesky, Baron.
What are taxes? / Baron Bedesky.
p. cm. -- (Economics in action)
Includes index.
ISBN-13: 978-0-7787-4262-3 (pbk. : alk. paper)
ISBN-10: 0-7787-4262-8 (pbk. : alk. paper)
ISBN-13: 978-0-7787-4257-9 (reinforced library binding : alk. paper)
ISBN-10: 0-7787-4257-1 (reinforced library binding : alk. paper)
1. Taxation--United States--Juvenile literature. 2. Taxation--Juvenile literature. I. Title. II. Series.
HJ2381.B395 2009
336.200973--dc22

2008025486

Contents

What are Taxes?

All people use **goods** and **services** every day. If they can touch items, they call them goods. If people hire other people to do work for them, they call it a service. A person's **wealth** not only includes his or her money, but his or her house, land, and possessions.

Introduction to Taxation

Our **government** manages many of these goods and services. Government consists of many people who work to give others the things they need the most. The term **economics** refers to the study of how both government and people manage money and resources.

A government manages the **economy** by using **taxation**. What is a **tax**? Taxes add an extra cost to the price of a purchase, and taxes take from the value of our **earnings** and possessions. A government charges taxes and uses this money to pay for all the services it offers. People agree to pay taxes to the government. In return, they receive many services designed to help make life easier and safer.

And what services does the government offer? City governments, for example, offer roads, sidewalks, stop lights, and city buses. They also build parks, schools, libraries, zoos, and airports. The money the government collects through taxes makes this all possible.

▼ Tax money paid to build Hoover Dam, which provides huge amounts of electricity to people in the U.S.

▲ Taxes pay for waste disposal so city streets stay clean.

The government also uses taxes as a tool to control what people spend. For example, the government may apply higher taxes on goods such as alcohol and cigarettes. The government hopes the taxes will stop people from using these unhealthy products. The government may also apply higher taxes to products made in other countries. This way American businesses can sell their goods for less money. This helps American companies.

Most of the time, people understand when they pay taxes. They receive a bill or receipt after they make a purchase. It clearly shows how much direct tax they paid. Sometimes, people do not know when they pay taxes. The seller may not tell the buyer about the tax. For example, telephone companies add taxes to the phone bills, and most customers are not aware of them. The company collects these hidden taxes and later pays them to the government.

FACT STOP

The word *tax* comes from a Latin word that means, "to touch." Centuries ago, tax collectors decided how much to take from people by examining what they owned. In many cases, this meant touching their items in order to decide on their value.

The History of Taxes

Humans have used taxes and tax collectors for thousands of years. As early as 6,000 years ago, people paid taxes in a land called Sumer located between the Tigris and Euphrates rivers in the area now known as Iraq. Recorded evidence shows tax collectors made their rounds at that time. The money paid for the cost of wars. It also paid for major irrigation projects for farmland.

▲ Some Egyptian art shows tax collectors collecting money for the Pharaohs.

Ancient Taxation

In Egypt, as early as 3000 B.C., evidence clearly shows people paid taxes. The tax collectors and inspectors at the time were called "scribes." The Egyptians taxed sales, businesses, farm crops, **imports**, and **exports**. Imports and exports refer to goods purchased from or delivered to other countries. The scribes went from business to business, farm to farm, and home to home to collect what the people owed.

Tax collectors had a lot of power in those ancient days. People both feared and hated them. Many tried to hide when the tax collectors made their rounds. The job of tax collecting could also be very dangerous. Sometimes, unhappy citizens who refused to pay would even beat or murder them.

King Henry VIII ruled England from 1509 to 1547. Early in his reign, he tried to make more money for his kingdom by increasing taxes, but the people protested and refused to pay. Looking for other ways to raise money, he announced that all the money collected by the Roman Catholic Church in England would go to him instead of to the Pope in Rome. Some people called it a tax on the church. Others described it as "the biggest heist of all time."

There are many such examples of taxation in history. Many times fair taxes helped the people, but just as often, high and unfair taxes hurt the people. History often shows how high taxes caused a government, a kingdom, or even an **empire** to crumble.

▲ King Henry VIII used taxes to raise money for his kingdom.

FACT STOP

Citizens in ancient Egypt often paid their taxes by working them off. The army drafted them and forced them into labor. People called this a **corvée**.

Taxes and the Revolution

The subject of taxes became one of the major reasons for the American Revolution from 1775 to 1783. The British government wanted the tax money to pay for the cost of defending the colonies. The colonists were upset because they had no say in the British government. They wanted colonists to look after their needs in the British Parliament.

Taxation Without Representation

The British announced a tax on sugar in the colonies in 1764 followed by the Stamp Act in 1765. The Stamp Act was a tax on legal papers, newspapers, and even playing cards. The Townshend Act in 1767 taxed the people for goods such as paper, glass, and tea. By now, many of the colonists grew so angry they refused to buy British goods.

Even with the tax, tea remained a very popular drink in the colonies. By 1773, however, most people refused to buy it from British suppliers. Instead, most tea arrived from Holland through colonists who refused to pay the tax. In an effort to sell more of their own tea, Britain passed the Tea Act in 1773. The act ended the tax on tea from British suppliers and allowed them to sell it for a much lower price than the Dutch tea.

▼ The 13 colonies in North America fought for independence in part because of the taxes that the British King charged them.

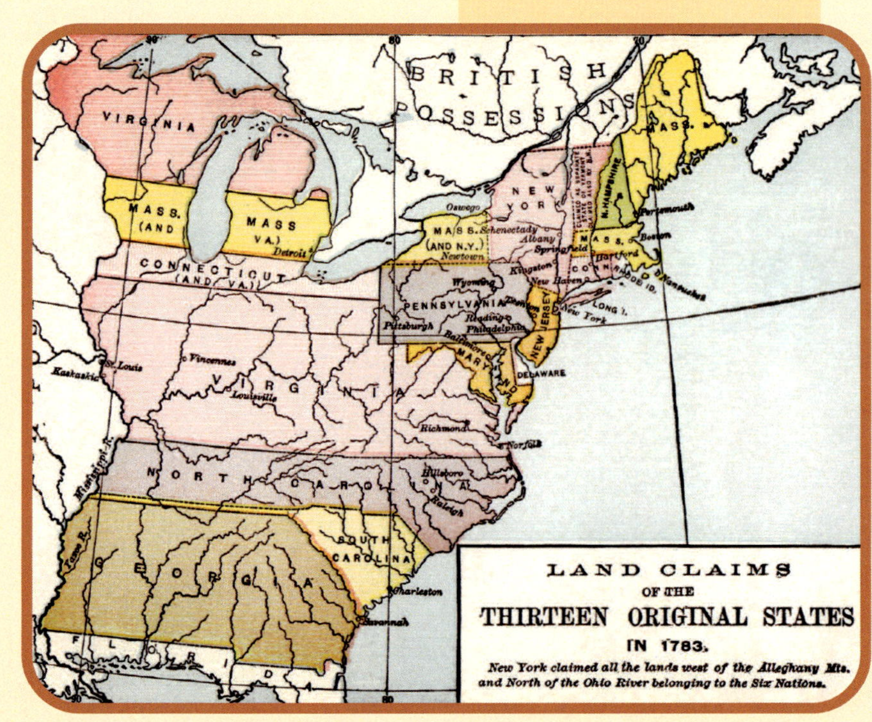

▲ The Boston Tea Party was a revolt against the taxes on tea from countries other than England.

This led to a famous event known as the Boston Tea Party. The first three ships with the cheaper British tea arrived at the Boston Harbor. The colonists demanded the ships return to England but they did not leave. On December 16, 1773, protesters boarded the ships in the harbor and dumped much of the tea into the water. This event created much support for the American Revolution.

While the revolution occurred, the new United States of America took shape. Many believed its new national government should not have the power to tax the people. After all, the new country formed when people objected to British taxes. A few years later, the leaders of the new country learned this would not work. The government could not manage the economy without tax money. By 1789, Congress began to tax Americans.

FACT STOP

The Boston Tea Party Ships and Museum honors one of the most famous events in American history. The Boston-based museum and three new model ships did not receive any tax money!

Taxes and the Civil War

One reason for the United States Civil War, which lasted from 1861 to 1865, had to do with taxes. This led to the Southern states forming their own government, which they called a Confederacy.

Taxes in the North and South

While slavery was a major reason for the conflict between the Confederate South and the Union North, the South also objected to high taxes. With a lower tax rate in place, the South believed it could attract a greater amount of world **trade**. It had major seaports in Charleston, South Carolina, Savannah, Georgia, and New Orleans, Louisiana. These seaports made it very simple to import and export goods.

The South's plan for low taxes made it very difficult to pay for the Civil War. Even if they did wish to raise taxes, the newly formed government would have had problems. It did not have a good system for collecting taxes. The Confederate government tried to sell war **bonds** to raise money. Few Southerners could afford the bonds.

▲ President Lincoln made sure the Union had enough money to fight the Civil War.

The South paid for the war by printing more Confederate money. The more money they printed, the less valuable it became. After a short time, Confederate money had no value.

The North decided to raise taxes. It already had an excellent tax-collection system in place and the money was quickly spent on the war effort. The North also sold war bonds to those who wished to help the Union against the Confederacy. The government expected that only the very rich would buy most of the bonds. It used a large **patriotic** advertising program to sell the bonds to all citizens. Many families purchased them even though they did not have much money.

As the war continued, the North decided to raise taxes for those who made the most money. This is **progressive** taxation. This extra money helped the North eventually defeat the South.

FACT STOP

The government eliminated most taxes after the Civil War. There were no longer any war costs to pay. The source of most tax **revenue** became liquor and tobacco taxes. **Income taxes** did not come back until 1913.

▼ When Confederate cities were destroyed, the South did not have money to rebuild.

Taxes Today - The Income Tax

Today, people pay taxes in many different ways. Income tax has become one of the most common taxes. People pay part of their earnings as income tax.

A Tax on What People Earn

Workers must file an income tax return once a year. They report how much money they earned during the year on a special form. People can calculate how much tax they owe based on how much they make. Sometimes a person will pay too much tax and they will receive a tax refund. Many others will not pay enough. Their forms will show they owe more taxes. Many people find it very confusing to properly complete their income tax forms. They often hire tax experts for help.

▼ Americans must file income tax forms every year to show they paid their share of taxes.

▲ The rich usually pay higher taxes than people with less money.

The first income tax law in the United States passed in 1861. The North needed a way to pay for the costs of the Civil War. The government eliminated the income tax in 1872. In 1913, the government passed the 16th Amendment to the **Constitution**. It allowed the federal government to collect an income tax.

Some people call income tax a progressive tax. This means those who earn more money pay a higher rate of tax. Those who earn less will pay a lower rate. The government uses a progressive tax because those who earn more money can afford to pay more tax. People with larger families may receive tax credits which can reduce the amount of income tax they pay. As of 2007, the income tax rate in the country ranged from ten percent to as high as 35 percent of a person's income. The amount paid depends on how much money a family makes. Currently, the five percent of the people who make the most money pay 60 percent of all income tax.

FACT STOP

Income taxes provide about five times as much money as taxes paid by businesses. This means individuals are paying for most of the services the government offers. Individuals also use and benefit the most from these services.

Sales Tax

A young person may believe they do not pay taxes because of their age. Only older people worry about taxes, right? Guess again. Anybody who buys something at their favorite store already pays taxes. They may not know it at the time, but they paid an extra amount called the sales tax.

A Tax for Shoppers

The seller adds sales tax to the price of many goods and services. People cannot avoid paying it as nearly every state uses them. Each state government decides what rate or percentage of tax it will charge. The rate applies to every store in that state. Many states do not add taxes to needs such as food or clothing.

Many people call sales taxes a **flat tax** or a **proportional tax**. Every person pays the same percentage. A poor person will pay the same rate of sales tax as a rich person. The rich person, however, can afford to buy more things. The more a person buys, the more tax they pay, but the rate always remains the same.

▼ Sales tax is added to the price of things that we buy.

▲ Every shopper in this store who buys something pays sales tax in addition to the price of what they purchase.

Other people call the sales tax a **regressive tax**. A regressive tax places a greater burden on the poor rather than the rich. People who do not make much money must pay the same tax as someone who makes a lot of money. A rich person will find it much easier to pay $500 in sales taxes in one year for groceries than a poor person will. Both may pay the same $500 because they both eat the same amount.

The sales tax rate often changes in different places in the same state. Local governments in counties and cities often add their own percentage to the state sales tax. The money raised helps these communities pay for the services they offer to people who live there. It also covers the cost of special projects in the community such as a new sports stadium.

FACT STOP

Alaska, Delaware, Montana, New Hampshire, and Oregon do not have state sales taxes. California has the highest state sales tax rate at 7.25 percent. California needs a higher tax because it has the largest population of any state.

Other Taxes

Some people must pay an **inheritance tax** if they receive money or property from someone who has passed away. They may also have to pay a gift tax if they are given a large amount of money or property. The amount of the tax depends on the value of the gift. The gift tax does not apply to smaller gifts people receive for birthdays or holidays.

Where Else do Taxes Come From?

Some companies pay a **tariff** for goods they buy from another country, but sell in their own country. A shoe factory in the United States may want to buy leather from another country because of the lower price. The United States government may add a tariff to raise the price of the imported leather. The shoe factory may then decide to buy the leather from a supplier in the United States. This helps protect businesses in the United States from competition around the world. Some countries such as Canada have a national goods and services tax. This extra sales tax gets added to the tax already charged by each province. This type of tax often angers people because it forces them to pay two taxes for one purchase.

Local governments will charge a yearly property tax to those who own land. This land may also have a home or a business on it. The amount of the tax depends on the value of the property. The government uses the money for services within that community or state.

▲ Businesses pay taxes on the land they own and money they make.

▲ Many states use toll roads. The money drivers pay to pass is a type of tax.

Businesses must pay a corporate tax. The amount depends on the **profit** the **corporation** makes in one year. A corporation calculates its profit after it subtracts all of its costs from all of its sales. The government charges different tax rates for different levels of profit. In the United States, the amount of corporate tax can be as low as 15 percent and as high as 39 percent. Many corporations make millions of dollars in profits each year. In 2006, these companies paid about 15 percent of the country's taxes.

Many people use highways, bridges, tunnels, and ferries. People who use these services must stop and pay a **toll** before they go on. The government uses the money it collects to repair or maintain these services. Many people like this type of tax. If they do not use these services, they do not have to pay the toll and share their cost.

FACT STOP

In some places, people call a toll road a *turnpike*. Long ago, long sticks called pikes blocked passage until people paid a toll. The pike would "turn," or open at a toll house after a traveler made a payment.

Taxes that Help

The government assists those over the age of 65, or senior citizens. As people get older, they may no longer be able to work. They still need money to live, though, so they receive Social Security payments from the government.

Money for the Aged

In 1935, the United States passed the **Social Security Act**. Both businesses and workers paid a small amount of their wages to the government. The government saved this money and began using it to help those too old to work. This money also helped those with disabilities, who cannot work due to illness and injury. Today, the government pays more money for Social Security than any other program. In 2004, the government spent nearly $500 billion dollars on Social Security! As the average age of Americans increases, the government will pay even more.

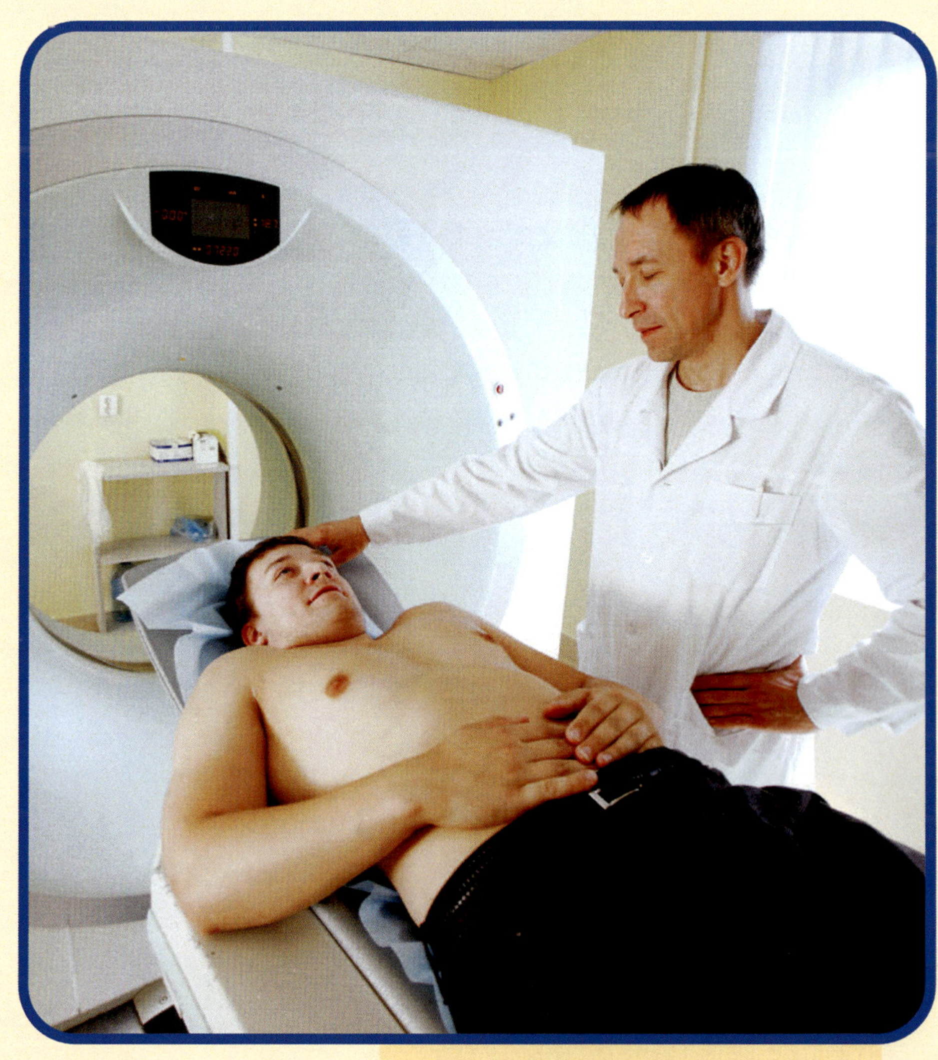

▲ Social Security can pay people who are too injured or ill to work.

▲ People aged 65 and older can receive Social Security payments.

In 1965, the United States government also created a program called **Medicare**. It helps those 65 years of age or older by paying some of their medical costs. This may include the cost of staying in a hospital. It covers the cost of seeing a doctor as well as medical tests such as x-rays. Medicare also helps many people younger than 65 who have disabilities.

Just like Social Security, the money for Medicare comes from both workers and businesses. Each pays a small amount of taxes to the government during the years someone earns a paycheck.

The government knows Medicare costs will quickly rise for the same reason Social Security will. The government pays over 40 cents of every dollar it receives to these two programs. The government spends less than half that amount on the military.

FACT STOP

President Lyndon Johnson signed Medicare into law in 1965. Former President Harry S. Truman received the first Medicare card. In 2007, more than 43 million people received Medicare.

Reasons for Taxation

The government uses taxation to serve many purposes. It's easy to remember those purposes by referring to the four Rs. They include revenue, **redistribution**, **re-pricing**, and **representation**.

Who Benefits from Taxes?

Revenue describes all the money a person or group receives. If someone earns money for working, that money is revenue. When people pay taxes, the government receives revenue. The government uses this revenue for the services it offers.

Redistribution means to take from one and give to the other. People who make more money also pay more taxes. The government uses much of that money for everyone in the country. The government also gives a lot of money to those who need help using programs like Social Security and Medicare. Taxes help redistribute money to those who need it most.

Governments also use taxes for re-pricing. It adds a tax to something to make it more expensive. Why would the government do this? Using tobacco as an example, the government adds extra tax to them to help stop people from smoking.

▲ Robin Hood stole from the rich and gave to the poor. The government takes more taxes from the rich. Often, the poor benefit.

▲ People who buy cars that use an extreme amount of gas pay a tax. This should encourage people to buy more energy-efficient cars.

The final R stands for representation. The word represent means "to serve." People want the government to serve them, especially if they give the government their tax dollars. If the people believe the government uses the money properly, they may decide to keep the same government. If the people feel the government did a poor job, they will elect new representatives.

Most people believe taxation helps everyone in the country. Yet most people also do not want high taxes. They will object if their taxes increase significantly over a short time. They will also object when asked for more taxes to help pay for a project they do not believe is necessary. For example, a county or city government may wish to raise local taxes to pay for a new sports stadium. Not everyone will agree that a new stadium will serve everyone's best interests. Sometimes, that government will give people the chance to vote whether or not to approve the new tax.

FACT STOP

When buying a bottle or a can of soda in Chicago, a person will pay a three percent tax. If they buy a soda served from a fountain, the tax goes up to nine percent!

Our Taxes at Work

The United States collected over $2.5 trillion dollars in taxes in 2006. What does the government do with all those tax dollars?

▲ Taxes pay for the people and equipment the United States military needs to protect the country.

What Do Taxes Pay For?

Taxes help pay for most of the schools in the country. The government works toward giving all children a chance to learn. It provides money for lunch programs. The government has also established guidelines to make sure the knowledge of all children meet certain minimum standards. It passed the "No Child Left Behind" Act in 2001. It promotes improving children's reading skills as well as the overall performance of all schools in the U.S.

The military protects the country. It also participates in important missions all over the world. Tax dollars pay all of the costs of the armed forces. It also pays for military bases and training.

Taxes pay for tunnels, bridges, pipelines, railroads, canals, and water treatment plants. Tax money covers the cost of making the bills and coins we use as money. Taxes also pay for the systems we need to provide electricity, and natural gas, as well as community housing projects.

Every government must have a **budget**. A budget helps a government plan how it will spend its money each year. A budget also determines the importance of projects. If a government spends more money than it planned, less important projects will not receive funding. Without a budget, a government may not spend its money responsibly. Sometimes a government may not spend all the money it has in the budget. This extra money can be saved for emergencies or unexpected extra expenses.

FACT STOP

The United States Congress spent more than 16 billion dollars on repairing and rebuilding houses damaged or destroyed by Hurricane Katrina in 2005. The project cost the government more money than any other housing project in American history.

▼ Tax money helps people after a natural disaster like a tornado or hurricane.

The Internal Revenue Service

The government has placed the **Internal Revenue Service** (IRS) in charge of collecting all taxes. The IRS searches for and charges those who do not obey the tax laws. As of 2006, 86,585 people worked for the IRS. Congress, the group of people in government who create federal laws, has only 535 people.

The Creation of the IRS

President Abraham Lincoln set up the first tax collection office in 1862. He became the first president to use an income tax in the United States. The program lasted from 1862 to 1872. The government of the North paid the costs of the Civil War using the money collected from income tax. When income taxes returned in 1913, the government used a different name. The government called it the Bureau of Internal Revenue. The government changed the name to the IRS in 1953.

▲ The Internal Revenue Service is known as the IRS.

Through the years, the IRS concentrated on catching those who cheated on their taxes. In the 1920s and early 1930s, Al Capone was a well-known gangster. The police were unable to charge him for any of his violent crimes. Capone was finally arrested and sent to jail for **tax evasion** in 1931.

▲ The Internal Revenue Service has offices all over the U.S.

Most people understand the importance of taxes. They know the government uses the money to pay for services to help everyone. Some people remain dishonest, though, and pay less tax money than they should.

When they find someone who lies in order to pay fewer taxes, the IRS has the power to **seize** their money or property. Today, most people provide the correct information on their income tax returns. No one wants to make a costly mistake. In 2006, the IRS started using companies to collect money from people who could not or would not pay their taxes.

The IRS performs an important job for the country. In 2006, it helped collect an amazing $2.5 trillion dollars from taxpayers. Nearly half of this came from individual income taxes. Taxes paid by employers amounted to more than $800 billion, while corporations paid $380 billion.

FACT STOP

In June, 2006, heavy rains caused a flood in the basement of the IRS offices in Washington, D.C. This caused big changes. Their offices moved into 15 other buildings around the city.

Choosing Not to Pay Taxes

People have objected to paying taxes for as long as taxes have existed. Some people disagree with taxes because they feel they should keep all of the money they earn. Others disagree with how the government spends the tax money. Even if they object, most people pay their taxes. A few people, however, choose not to pay.

Tax Evasion

The term tax evasion describes an act in which a person does not pay all the taxes the tax laws say is owed. Tax evasion can also mean a person has not completed their tax return. In 2007,the IRS stated that tax evasion resulted in about $345 billion of unpaid taxes.

▼ Some people try to **smuggle**, or sneak, expensive items into the U.S. to keep from paying taxes on them.

People may receive a penalty of up to one year in jail and a $25,000 fine for each year they did not file a tax return. Those who file incorrect information on their tax return can spend up to three years in jail and pay up to $100,000 in fines. Others intentionally plan not to pay any or most of their taxes. They may receive the greatest punishment and spend up to five years in jail and pay up to $100,000 in fines.

They do this to confuse the IRS if it ever decides to examine their records to make sure they are correct. If the IRS suspects that someone is not being honest or paying all of the taxes owed, they might ask to examine the person's records. The IRS calls such an examination an **audit**.

Many people bring goods into the United States from another country. They must report their purchases, and in certain cases, pay a tax when they return to the United States. The government applies this tax to prevent people from bringing in large amounts of cheaper products from another country instead of buying them in the United States. If they do not report them, the government may charge them with smuggling.

FACT STOP

The courts sentenced movie star Wesley Snipes to three years in jail in 2008 for failing to file many of his income tax returns to the government.

▼ When people feel they are forced to pay too much tax, they may protest.

The Future of Taxes

Both the government and the people wish to find a way of improving the system of taxation. The government wants to eliminate tax evasion. The people want the government to spend tax money wisely. The government passes tax laws to reach these goals.

Tax Reform

The government also uses taxes to manage the economy. Adding or removing certain taxes can encourage people to use their money to help the economy. Many people want to change and work toward tax **reform**.

Tax reforms may call for a change to how much tax people pay. They could also change how the government uses tax revenue. Congressman John Linder of Georgia has suggested the **Fair Tax**. His plan would eliminate all income tax, payroll tax, corporate tax, gift tax and inheritance tax. He suggests a sales tax of 23 percent on all goods and services.

▶ U.S. Representative John Linder sponsored the Fair Tax. The Fair Tax would eliminate the IRS.

▲ The government can use taxes to create and maintain beautiful national parks.

The government promises to review the Fair Tax reforms. So far, they have received more support in Congress than any other tax reform in recent history. Using a Fair Tax would probably result in the elimination of the IRS and that would save tax payers hundreds of millions of dollars. It would also cost thousands of IRS people their jobs so the Fair Tax does have some disadvantages.

Another tax reform gaining in popularity suggests the elimination of the federal tax on gasoline. This tax would save Americans 18.4 cents per gallon of gas they buy.

FACT STOP

The average U.S. family with two children pays a tax rate of 11.9 percent. Families of the same size in Turkey pay 42.7 percent. Families in Sweden also pay a very high 42.4 percent. Families in Ireland pay a very low tax of 8.1 percent.

Glossary

audit To examine the financial reports of a person or business

bond A certificate sold by government to people to help raise funds

budget A plan showing how money is earned and spent

constitution The laws and rules used to govern a state or country

corporation A business managed by a group of people and owned by shareholders

corvée Being forced to serve or work to pay a debt to government

earnings The total amount of money made by a person or business

economics Science of limited resources

economy The system used to manage goods and services

empire An alliance of different groups of people joined under one leader

exports Goods made in one country and delivered to other countries

Fair Tax A suggested simple tax to replace many other complicated taxes

flat tax A tax charge that is the same for everyone

goods Products or merchandise bought and sold by businesses and people

government A group of people chosen by others who manage and lead a community

imports Goods received by one country but made in other countries

income tax Tax taken from what a person is paid for their work

inheritance tax Tax on goods received from those who have died

Internal Revenue Service A government agency in charge of collecting all of the country's taxes

Medicare A government plan to help the elderly with their health care costs

patriotic An action that occurs out of love and support for a country

profit The extra money left after expenses are subtracted from income

progressive Taxation in which those with more money pay more tax

proportional tax A tax only added when someone uses or buys something

redistribution Taking from one person or place and giving it to another

reform Making something better by changing it

regressive tax Taxation in which those with less money pay more tax

representation The act of serving other people or doing as they ask

re-pricing Changing the cost of goods or services to affect buying and selling

revenue Money received by a person, a business, or the government

seize To take from a person or a business

services Work that is completed by one or more people for the benefit of others

smuggle To hide imported or exported goods to avoid paying taxes or tariffs

Social Security Act A government plan to financially help the elderly and unemployed

tariff A tax on goods imported to or exported from a country

tax An extra cost on goods and services collected by government

tax evasion Acting in a way to avoid paying tax as required by law

taxation The way a government manages taxes in a community or country

toll An amount paid to use a route for transportation

trade Buying and selling between people, communities, or countries

wealth The total value of all things owned by a person or people

Index

Webfinder

http://bensguide.gpo.gov/
www.kids.gov
www.ssa.gov/kids/kids.htm
www.kidsbank.com
www.factmonster.com
www.worldalmanacforkids.com